7 Steps to Finding Your Spiritual Life

7 Steps to Finding Your Spiritual Life

Previously published as Public Spirituality: A Personal Workbook

Lisa Langford Heron
Brian Langford Heron, M. Div.

*Michelle —
Best wishes —
Lisa Langford*

iUniverse, Inc.
New York Lincoln Shanghai

7 Steps to Finding Your Spiritual Life

iUniverse books may be ordered through booksellers or by contacting:

iUniverse
2021 Pine Lake Road, Suite 100
Lincoln, NE 68512
www.iuniverse.com
1-800-Authors (1-800-288-4677)

The nature of spiritual exploration naturally leads to addressing and exposing the deepest parts of our lives. The questions in this workbook may bring to the surface painful memories and unresolved issues (such as childhood trauma, abuse, abandonment, violence or victimization, unresolved grief or loss). Nothing on The Center for Public Spirituality's web site or in this workbook is intended to replace the clinical expertise of trained therapists, psychologists, and psychiatrists. In the event that significant unresolved issues arise during the course of working through this workbook, you are advised to seek professional help.

ISBN-13: 978-0-595-34205-1 (pbk)
ISBN-13: 978-0-595-78975-7 (ebk)
ISBN-10: 0-595-34205-1 (pbk)
ISBN-10: 0-595-78975-7 (ebk)

Printed in the United States of America

Contents

Introduction

*The most important thing in
defining spirit is the recognition
that spirit is an essential need of
human nature. There is something
in all of us that seeks the spiritual.*

Rachel Naomi Remen, M.D.

America is the most religiously diverse nation on the planet. Although the majority of Americans claim Christianity as their religion, we also have 5 million Buddhists, 6 million Jews, and 7 million Muslims. These, in addition to Hindus, Native Americans, Wiccans, Pagans, Unitarian Universalists, Religious Scientists, and hundreds of other religious groups, are all part of America's religious diversity.

And this is just a picture of America's *religious* diversity. While half of all Americans are part of a faith community another 25 percent identify with a particular religion, but don't claim membership in any community. The remaining 25 percent of Americans claim no religious affiliation and think of themselves in either spiritual or secular terms.

Among Americans there is an incredibly broad range of spiritual expression. There are people who see themselves in completely religious terms and those who see themselves solely in secular terms. In between there are people exploring and mixing and matching spiritual beliefs and practices. People experiment with two, three, even four different religions during the course of a lifetime. A great number of people are beginning to design their own spirituality completely away from organized religion.

If one line captures the changing dynamic of America's relationship with religion it is this: "I'm more spiritual than religious." I have heard that comment hundreds of times over the past fifteen years. Couples seeking wedding services said it wanting to make sure I honored their unique spiritual beliefs in the wedding ceremony. Adult children of church members often explained why they didn't attend church saying, "I am not really religious, but I am spiritual." In the broader community, people often revealed the same thing as they discovered my role as a minister.

At first I thought this comment represented a dividing line between those who were members of a faith community and those who weren't. I thought it was a wall separating those whose identity was grounded in a religion from those who had a more secular identity. I no longer think that.

What I have discovered is that people meet their spiritual needs in a variety of ways. In my early years of ministry, I assumed that people came to church primarily because of their beliefs, to define and articulate their worldview. I assumed this because that is largely why I was part of a faith community. I was surprised by people who didn't care one way or another about what I preached, but who regularly showed up for church because these were "their people." They came out of a spiritual need to belong to a community. I discovered many people came on Sundays because I was preaching on a certain topic and others who never missed a Communion Sunday. The former were looking for insight into their Christian life. The latter came out of a need for the grounding presence of ritual and tradition. Some members came to church as the one place where they could express their compassion in a competitive world. Others came for spiritual renewal after spending all week in compassionate professions. I learned that people came to church for many different reasons.

In recent years I have served the community in social services, law enforcement, and hospice. I have discovered that people are extremely creative in how they meet their basic spiritual needs. Many, of course, do belong to faith communities. But just as many are out there meeting their spiritual needs by picking and choosing from a variety of religious, spiritual, and secular resources. I work with people who identify themselves as fundamentalist Christians, atheists, Buddhists, liberal Christians, Bahai, Unitarian Universalists, humanists, and agnostics. I work with those exploring Wiccan beliefs, Native American spiritualities, as well as Islamic and Hindu practices.

Despite the variety, I have discovered that a basic yearning for spiritual meaning in our lives unites us. We all seek to give meaning to our lives, feel a sense of purpose, and understand our connection to the world around us. Some of us satisfy this yearning through traditional religious means, some through more general spiritual approaches, and still others through completely secular avenues. We may satisfy our spiritual yearnings in diverse ways, but we are unified in having the same basic spiritual needs.

This book is intended to articulate our common spiritual needs while honoring the unique ways we each seek to meet our spiritual needs. Since the September 11, 2001, terrorist attacks, there may be no better time to commit to this work—honoring our diversity as well as that which connects us.

This Workbook and Spirituality

This workbook acts as an introduction to spirituality, defining and describing spirituality in terms of individual spiritual and religious expression. As a tool for personal exploration, whether or not you are affiliated with an organized religion, the workbook is a way to become familiar with your own religious and spiritual practices and identity.

The language used here to discuss spirituality describes seven areas or domains of spiritual life that provide a basic spiritual foundation. This way of talking about spirituality validates the importance of each person's individual spiritual expression. People using this language have deepened their understanding of their own spirituality, both within and apart from organized religion.

Each person can bring his or her own individual religious and spiritual practices, beliefs, insights, and experiences into this language of spirituality. In addition, using the language of spirituality creates an effective, positive, and nonjudgmental, shared context in which to discuss religion and spirituality with others.

Defining terms

Let's define some terms:

> **Spirituality** is the way people describe their relationship to the whole, their relationship to that which brings meaning, purpose, and connection into their lives.

> **Spiritual Life** is how each person lives out his spirituality, including practices, beliefs and activities that support his spirituality.

> **Spiritual Practice** describes anything anyone does that enhances her spirituality. It often includes a level of discipline and intention. Followers of one religion are more likely to have similar spiritual practices because their religion is guiding them. People not associated with a particular religion are more likely to have a variety of practices incorporated in their lives to meet their spiritual needs.

> **Religion** is a set of spiritual practices and beliefs that is held in common by a larger community and that people follow to meet their spiritual needs. Many people find that some parts of the religion are vital parts of their spirituality. These religious (i.e., specific) practices are part of their spiritual (i.e., general) practice.

Before reading any further, take the following assessment. The goal of this assessment is to give you an accurate snapshot of your satisfaction with your spiritual life.

Think about your life. This assessment reflects how satisfied you are with each area. There is no judgment here. Your experience is your experience, and as such is valid. As you take the assessment, gently and honestly reflect on your own life and experiences.

Ready?

The Assessment

For each question, rank your level of satisfaction with a number from 1 to 10. A score of 1 represents very low satisfaction while a score of 10 represents a high level of satisfaction. Remember that this is *your* perception and *your* sense of satisfaction with these areas of your life.

Section I

How satisfied are you with

_____1. The presence of compassion in your closest relationships?

_____2. The amount of time and energy you feel you can commit to compassionate activities on behalf of others?

_____3. Your openness and ability to accept help from others in your times of need?

Section II

How satisfied are you with

_____4. Your chosen beliefs and values to guide you through life?

_____5. How well your beliefs are integrated into your daily living?

_____6. Your ability to live your life in keeping with your deepest values?

Section III

How satisfied are you with

_____7. Your sense of purpose and meaning for your life?

_____8. The feeling that you have gifts and abilities that benefit others?

_____9. The amount of time and energy you spend in activities that give you meaning, pleasure, and a sense of accomplishment?

Section IV

How satisfied are you with

_____10. The amount of unscheduled, relaxing time in your life?

_____11. How much you engage in reflection and contemplation (meditation, prayer, yoga, silent walks, etc.)?

_____12. Your sense of connection to the most sacred part of life (God, soul, true Self, ground of being, source of life, higher power, The Force, etc.)?

Section V

How satisfied are you with

_____13. The level of tradition in your life that ties you to those closest to you and to your community?

_____14. The rituals in your life to convey a sense of spiritual meaning during life transitions?

_____15. Your ability to honor and commemorate meaningful events in your own life?

Section VI

How satisfied are you with

_____16. Your ability to keep mind/body/spirit in harmony and balance?

_____17. The amount of time you spend in deeply pleasurable activities (music, massage, enjoyment of food, sexual intimacy, being in nature)?

_____18. Your body, its rhythms, and your physical activities?

Section VII

How satisfied are you with

_____19. The amount of acceptance you feel from those most important to you?

_____20. Your comfort in sharing your thoughts, feelings, ideas, and opinions with those closest to you?

_____21. The level of honesty, trust, and commitment in your relationships?

In each section of three questions, add your scores. For example, if for question 1 you scored your satisfaction level at a 7, and for question 2 you scored your satisfaction level at a 6, and for question 3 you scored your satisfaction level at an 8, then your total score for that section would be 21.

List your totals for each of the sections.

Section I	_____	Compassion
Section II	_____	Worldview
Section III	_____	Vocation
Section IV	_____	Sacred Space
Section V	_____	Ritual and Tradition
Section VI	_____	Harmony with Nature
Section VII	_____	Community

The highest possible score in a section is 30; the lowest is 3.

Each section represents a domain, or area of your spiritual life, or spiritual practice. The words *domain* and *area* are used interchangeably to describe each of the seven separate aspects of your spiritual life described in this book.

Fulfilling Spiritual Practice

Whether part of a religious institution or not, your spiritual practice should provide a healthy, satisfying, and balanced spiritual life. Spiritual practice should guide you toward a life of *meaning* and *purpose* and foster a sense of *connection*.

Seven Domains of Spiritual Practice

The domains of spiritual practice, present in every major religion as well as in the most secular among us, include:

1. **Compassion:** the giving and receiving of caring and kindness
2. **Worldview:** the integration of your life experiences, values, and beliefs
3. **Vocation:** the exploration of your purpose in life
4. **Sacred space:** connecting with your deepest self, your soul, or God
5. **Ritual and tradition:** marking life passages and honoring your identity
6. **Harmony with nature:** honoring our physical natures
7. **Community:** honoring our connection with others

Identifying these seven domains allows us to recognize, acknowledge, and honor our spirituality whether within religious settings or within less traditional spiritual practices.

Unique Lives, Unique Spiritual Practices

There is not one way to live a healthy spiritual life. Every life is so unique that it is impossible to present one spiritual life formula and have it fit everyone. People's personalities, preferences, experiences, and religious and spiritual backgrounds are so diverse that each person needs to determine the appropriate balance for each area of his or her spiritual life.

Stress, different stages of life, and life circumstances will affect your satisfaction and needs in each area. It may be helpful to retake the assessment periodically as a personal check-in, as changes in your life may result in changes in your spiritual practices.

Nutrition as Metaphor

Understanding how to deal with spirituality is similar to understanding how we deal with nutritional needs. Every human being on the planet has nutritional needs.

We also know that many different foods are eaten around the world to meet these basic nutritional needs. Cultures, families, and individuals eat different foods to meet their nutritional needs. By recognizing our shared need for basic nutrition, we can identify and appreciate the different ways nutritional needs are met.

Spirituality is no different. This book describes seven domains or areas of spiritual life. Addressing these seven domains is like addressing the amount of protein and calories in our diet. The seven domains are basic human spiritual needs. Recognizing that these are universal and basic spiritual needs is the first step in starting to examine how well we are meeting these needs.

Using the nutrition analogy, we know that we get our necessary protein and calories in different ways based on what our culture offers, what our family ate, as well as our own individual preferences.

Spiritually, our necessary elements are addressed in different ways as well, based on our culture, the family we grew up in, and our own individual preferences.

Two Necessary Ingredients

In formulating a plan for optimal spiritual well-being, two ingredients are helpful. The first is becoming familiar with basic elements involved in spiritual practice. The second is to know yourself.

This book does both. It identifies and defines seven basic domains or areas of spiritual life. This book also helps you discover your preferences, tendencies, and possibilities so you can recognize and embrace a spiritual life that will work for you.

Your Spiritual Practice

Your spiritual practice is just that—*yours*. Becoming more aware of specific areas in your spiritual life, you can become more intentional about how you incorporate each area into your life as well as how much or how little time you spend with each area. We urge you to pay attention to your inner voice, which some people call God, which may be urging you to address a certain area.

How to Use This Book

Each chapter presents an opportunity for you to explore specific areas of your spiritual life and can be taken independently. The book can also be read straight through, based on your interest and desires. Some people find that working through all the chapters gives them a fuller understanding of their spiritual life.

The assessment is repeated in Chapter 8. It is offered there to give you an opportunity to take it again after you've read through and done the work in each of the chapters. Notice any change in your satisfaction in any of the areas.

Chapters 1 through 7 contain three sections apiece. Each chapter begins with a description of Lisa's experience with the domain. The second section describes and defines the domain. The final, most important section gives you an opportunity to explore and write down your experiences.

Take time for this process. Don't rush through the book. Use the space provided to journal your responses to the questions. Your responses are a reflection of your unique spiritual practices, whether you are part of a religious institution or not.

You may be surprised at how many ways you are already addressing your spirituality!

CHAPTER 1

Compassion

*There is nothing heavier than
compassion. Not even one's own
pain weighs so heavy as the pain one
feels with someone, for someone, a
pain intensified by the imagination
and prolonged by a hundred echoes.*

Milan Kundera

One of the most significant gifts of compassion I received was one that the giver may not even remember.

I was having a horrible day. I don't even remember what it was that made that particular day so awful. Brian had gone to visit a couple who were new to the church. I'd met and liked them, but we hadn't had time yet to develop a friendship. During his visit with them, he'd told them that I was having a rough time.

Within a few hours, Cathy was at my door with a batch of brownies, telling me she was thinking about me and hoping things would get better.

I almost cried. Someone else had known of my pain and thought about me. A busy working mother, she still took a few hours to do something nice for me—a person she didn't even know very well. I knew she understood what it was like to have a bad day. I felt understood and cared for on a deep level.

It speaks to the power of compassion that I can't remember specifically what made the day so awful, yet I can remember the compassion that helped me through it.

Defining Compassion

Compassion is a transforming ingredient for a healthy spiritual practice. Just as flour and water are transformed into bread by the presence of yeast, a self-serving practice is transformed into a truly spiritual practice by the presence of compassion.

Compassion is an act of solidarity with another. It is a genuine reaching out with the best of what you have to give.

Compassion means literally "to suffer with." It runs deeper than acts of charity, which see the "needy and poor" or the "stuffy and rich" as separate, and often engender pity or jealousy rather than genuine empathy.

Religious leaders and sacred writings have often addressed compassion and kindness as the central precept of religion. The Hindu leader Basavanna says, "What sort of religion can it be without compassion? You need to show compassion to all living beings. Compassion is the root of all religious faiths."

Compassion is being in tune with those we encounter every day, understanding and reaching out with what we have to give. Compassion is also being in tune with our own needs, including being able to ask for and receive the support and help of others. It reveals our connectedness as we nurture our ability to reach out to others and allow others to reach out to us.

Compassion can be cooking a meal for someone in need, listening when someone needs to be heard, doing a chore for someone who cannot, forgiving someone, offering a gift to someone new, or sending a note of concern when someone is suffering. Compassion can also be found in parenting, relationships with friends and family, as well as in casual relationships, caring for animals, and caring for the planet.

Many people's life work (vocation) is borne out of compassion. Compassion can be found in working with underprivileged children, those who are sick and dying, the imprisoned, the lonely, the impoverished, and the disenfranchised.

Compassion doesn't have to be huge gestures of life sacrifice or monetary gifts, although, of course, it can be. Compassion is most often found in intimate relationships with family and friends. Genuine compassion is borne out of the innate sense of connection we have with our fellow human beings.

Your Exploration

Use the space given to explore *compassion* in your life.

Which religious teachings (sacred texts, prophets, spiritual/religious leaders, clergy/clerics, rabbis) taught you about compassion?

You have probably learned about compassion from other sources as well (which would then be considered spiritual sources): novels, movies, poetry. **List other sources that have taught you about compassion.**

People in our lives also teach us about compassion—some through their words, others through their actions.

Think of the people you have known and how they have used their own gifts, talents, and interests to live compassionately (cooking, fixing things, listening, reading, caregiving, prayer, etc.).

Who in your life taught you about compassion through their actions?

What do you admire about the people you know who live out their compassion?

Compassion often feels like a natural extension of who you are, truly becoming a gift from the heart.

Think about your own gifts, talents, and interests.
List how you use your gifts to express compassion to others.

How have you used your life to express compassion?

Specifically, how do you *best* express compassion to others?

Compassion is not just about giving and doing for others. Receiving compassion is just as important as giving it. Sometimes the compassionate thing to do is to accept compassion from others to rejuvenate ourselves when we're depleted.

Who has shown compassion to you? (Think of friends, parents, grandparents, coworkers, neighbors, even strangers.)

How have they shown compassion? (Have they listened, cooked/prepared/bought food, flowers/plants, forgiven you, provided caregiving for you or someone close to you, provided a service, monetary help?)

What is the most meaningful act of compassion you've received from someone else?

How did you feel about receiving such a wonderful gift?

Our lives are rich with compassion.
A small child expresses compassion when he gives his teddy bear
to his sad parent.
A friend watches a parent's children, showing compassion for
the overburdened parent.
A community provides meals for the homeless.
A woman mows her elderly neighbor's lawn.
A coworker sends a supportive e-mail.
Money is collected for the families of disaster victims.
A hand is clasped in comfort. A loving look.
A listening ear. A gentle touch.

CHAPTER 2

Worldview

And in Bible-story journeys,
ain't no journey hopeless.
Everybody find what they suppose to find.

Sounder, *William H. Armstrong*

When I first accepted fundamentalist beliefs in college, I felt as though I was supposed to accept them unconditionally, as though by merely accepting them my spiritual journey was complete. Yet as life went on, I found that the beliefs I'd embraced didn't stand up to close scrutiny or questions. Brian's studies in seminary as well as just living life brought more questions and further exploration, as well as more complex answers.

Rather than divorcing myself from the questions and the life that brought them, I embraced the questions and the exploration. Learning, studying, thinking about faith and spiritual and religious issues continued to be a focus for me. Some of this exploration seemed opposed to many of the fundamentalist beliefs I'd accepted earlier.

Studying faith issues at the Presbyterian seminary Brian attended (and I absorbed vicariously) made me feel as though I was coming back to my Presbyterian roots with a deeper, more meaningful understanding of them. My beliefs changed, yes; but they were broadened and deepened. I felt as if I were then able to believe with my whole being.

Worldview is perhaps the most fundamental ingredient of a spiritual practice. It is such an integral part of who you are that it may be a challenge to step back and recognize it.

Defining Worldview

While our life events, beliefs, and physical and emotional needs are often similar to those of others, each of us comes to a unique understanding of the world. No one person's combination of personality, beliefs, values, and life experiences is exactly the same as anyone else's.

From *The User's Guide to the Brain*, by John J. Ratey, M.D.:

> The key thing to remember is that each newborn must create its own particular understanding of the world, and that each individual throughout life continually reinforces, adds to, and sometimes changes his view of the world. It is not uncommon, for example, for people who have had a heart attack or other trauma to throw out their old view of life and take on a new one. A math professor who becomes increasingly fascinated with art and increasingly bored with his job may one day throw out his books and eventually become an accomplished artist. The development of values that drive the evolution of consciousness may also explain how two people can view the same circumstances so differently: a citizen sees the

gunning down of a crime boss in a restaurant as terrible; the gunman sees it as an act essential to his crime family's survival.

From the very beginning, we develop views about the nature of the world and our place in it, whether we are conscious of this process or not.

Religions present worldviews. Each religion presents its own particular views or ideas about God, death, and what happens after death, whether the world is a good place, and whether human beings are good, evil, or redeemable.

For example, a Christian view is that there is a savior of mankind, Jesus. A Buddhist view is that nirvana (enlightenment) is attained by the removal of all separateness; it is the state of complete non-attachment. A central view of Judaism is that the Jewish people are chosen and serve one God. These basic perspectives and beliefs inform the thoughts, ideas, and actions of the followers.

Religious experiences, life experiences, upbringing (cultural, family, economic status), personality, beliefs, and values all meld within individuals to form a unique and distinct view of the world.

Your upbringing played a huge part in determining your worldview. Whether abusive or nurturing, supportive or punitive, your upbringing has helped shaped your view of the world and you.

The worldviews of people who were important in your childhood (parents, siblings, relatives, teachers, religious/spiritual leaders, friends) influenced you. The values and beliefs and messages from your upbringing are part of you still. Whether you have consciously repudiated those views or unconsciously incorporated them into your life, these values have been part of you and shape who you are.

Your Exploration

The next sections present three areas for you to explore. The first area is your *beliefs*, which are those tenets you accept as true. The second area is your *values*, or those qualities you consider desirable. The third area offers an opportunity for you to explore your *life experiences*.

Allow this chapter to be an opportunity for you to honor and recognize what went into the development of your worldview, that which makes you who you are today.

Beliefs

Use the space provided to explore your worldview and how it developed.

Before you answer the questions, think about the beliefs important in your upbringing as well as what you believe now. Honor your experience by allowing yourself to respond with whatever comes. There are no incorrect answers.

Look at the topics (this is not an inclusive list):

God	love
death	forgiveness
good and evil	the Bible
pain and suffering	the Koran (Qur'an)
sin	the Torah
humanity	Upanishads
redemption	spirituality
sexuality	religion
atonement	violence
women's place in the world	men's place in the world
heaven	hell
what it means to be grown up	human nature
family	wholeness

While you may be familiar with different religious and spiritual traditions and how they represent God, good and evil, death, growing up, and a multitude of other issues, you have your own beliefs.

Choose three topics from the list. Complete the following set of three questions using the three topics you chose.

Topic #1 _____ (write in your first topic from the list here)

What I learned from my upbringing about _____was

What I believe now about _____is

Topic #2 _____ (write in your second topic here)

What I learned from my upbringing about _____was

What I believe now about _____is

Topic #3 _____ (write in your third topic here)

What I learned from my upbringing about _____was

What I believe now about _____is

Complete each sentence, thinking about your beliefs.

The beliefs from my upbringing that I most embrace in my life now are

The beliefs from my upbringing that I most reject are

Values

Think about the values important in your upbringing and what you value now. As you look at the list of values, notice the values that attract you and seem appealing to you, as well as those you find disagreeable.

Look at these values (again, this is not an inclusive list):

fun	kindness	understanding
power	winning	autonomy
hard work	empathy	competence
strong relationships	sexual excitement	prestige
bravery	honesty	leisure
being superior	wealth	being funny
teaching	acquiring things	sharing
exploration	loyalty	security
risk-taking	fidelity	being in control
originality	companionship	independence
being right	integrity	creativity
humor	punctuality	aesthetics
intelligence	discovery	self-expression
devotion	commitment	hearing others
comfort	caring for those less fortunate	excitement

Think about the values in the list. Pay attention to values that invoke strong feelings. They can be values you are attracted to or ones you are not attracted to. Complete each set of questions using values you chose.

Complete each sentence, thinking about your values.

Three values that I most embrace in my life now are

    1.

    2.

    3.

Three values that I most reject are

    1.

    2.

    3.

Life Experiences

Not only do our beliefs and values inform our worldview, but our life experiences also can influence how we view the world and how it works.

Every experience we have is integrated into how we understand the world. Yet while everything we have ever experienced is incorporated into our view of the world, most of the events/experiences are so minute we hardly notice them.

There are, however, events that affect our lives profoundly, so much so that they dramatically change how we view the world. Events we experience in our lives can change our view of God (or no God), our political views, and how we view humanity. Just as events can change our beliefs, events can also confirm views of the world we already hold, perhaps making our beliefs stronger.

Think about significant events in your life (births, deaths, wars, traumas, natural disasters, significant losses or gains, illnesses, recoveries, religious influences, relationships).

Remember significant events in your life. Allow yourself to remember your thoughts and feelings about the event as well as how it changed or confirmed your views.

In this space name at least three events that have been significant in your life.

1.

2.

3.

Think about each significant event you listed separately. Write down how each event has influenced your thinking, your beliefs, and values. (Has it strengthened them, challenged them, changed them, confirmed them?)

1. Event _____
Affected my beliefs and values

2. Event _____
Affected my beliefs and values

3. Event _____
Affected my beliefs and values

Our worldviews are being shaped continually.
As we grow and develop—physically, emotionally, cognitively,
and spiritually—our world expands.
We become aware of issues and ideas we hadn't known about before.
We learn and think.
Life unfolds.
Worldviews deepen and change.

CHAPTER 3

Vocation

I'm doing what I was made to do.

Billy Tyne, A Perfect Storm

As soon as I learned how to read and write, I kept journals, wrote letters, expressed opinions, and discovered things through the writing. I learned about myself through writing, processed feelings through writing, and shared myself with others through writing. School was wonderful because writing was a huge part of it.

My first child was born when I was twenty-five. I didn't write, being too tired, too consumed by caring for an infant, doing laundry, cooking, cleaning, and trying to keep a little money coming in while Brian was in seminary. I told myself there wasn't time to write anything.

Seminary continued, we had another child, and I still wasn't writing.

Then Brian decided to become a pastor. I didn't question that decision or how it might affect me. We moved to Wisconsin into a difficult church situation. I felt thrust into a role I didn't want (a pastor's wife), and felt lonely and isolated in a city not particularly welcoming to newcomers. I got really angry. I raged for over a year, seemingly from every pore.

Then, in a short, quick urge, I started writing poetry. I discovered that it helped me work through some of my feelings and thoughts, helped me articulate, and therefore validate my feelings at a time when I wasn't feeling validated for very much. Writing poetry became a way for me to capture a thought or a feeling on paper. After writing the poem, I could let the feeling go.

Through my poems, I was able to reconnect with myself.

Writing brings me joy. It helps me; it allows me to express myself. It is my vital life work, my vocation.

I've realized that in the past I've let the writing go, telling myself that life is too hectic, or it isn't important enough.

It *is* important enough. I need to make it a priority. There will always be more people and things pulling at me that could take me away from writing. I've had to learn how to say no, and to make room in my life for writing.

This became hard for me when I had children. Before that, time for writing was just there. I was always able to find time to write; and often because it was assigned in school, I was supposed to write. Having small children, teaching school, and working in a social service agency have been consuming endeavors for me. I can't give everything I have to the kids or at the office. Knowing my boundaries and setting limits so I have time for writing was something I had to learn.

When we use our unique talents and passions and feel that "this is what I was made for," then we are living our vocation.

Defining Vocation

Author Shakti Gawain describes work this way, "Work and play are the same. When you are following your energy and doing what you want all the time, the distinction between work and play dissolves."

Sam Keen, in his book *Hymns to an Unknown God*, defines vocation as having four components. If it is to be a genuine vocation, you must have a *gift* for it, you must have the *discipline* to pursue it, it must give you *delight* to do it, and there must be a *need* for it in the world.

Religions have used the word *vocation* to talk about a "calling" to a particular religious life. Traditionally, being "called" has meant being "called" for a specifically religious vocation, such as religious leadership, or monastic life, or missionary life.

Some people have felt "called" to a particular field of study or career path that is not specifically religious. In some larger spiritual way, they have known that their chosen field or work was what they needed to be doing with their lives. Your vocation is what you are "called" to do, whether or not it is to a traditionally religious life.

Living your vocation may be your job or career, though it may just as easily be something that takes place outside of work. Hobbies you love, working with your hands, a sport or group activity, fixing things, reading and writing, writing letters, collecting and learning about things (rocks, stamps, etc.) may be your vocation. Relationships you nurture or roles you live, such as parenting, may be your vital life work. Your vocation may be borne out of life circumstances or out of compassion. Doctors, nurses, and caregivers may be living out their vocation.

People living out their vocation, their vital life work, deeply enjoy most of the time they spend doing it. They lose track of time. They become engrossed.

Some people know their vocation at a very young age. Others discover their vocation later in life—sometimes through gifts, talents, or opportunities not recognized earlier.

Your Exploration

Using the space provided, record your responses to the questions.

Think about things you love to do. When you are engaged in these activities, you lose track of time and are completely engrossed. You feel as though your creativity and best self are being engaged. Gardening, writing, crafting, fixing/building things, organizing accounting, making music, and being in a relationship may be among the activities you enjoy on a deep level.

Name at least five things you do that bring you deep fulfillment and joy.

1.

2.

3.

4.

5.

Think about the activities that are important to you, the activities you want to make a priority in your life. There are activities (interests, endeavors) you want to nurture, even if only for small amounts of time.

Name at least five activities you want to allow time for in your life.

1.

2.

3.

4.

5.

Sometimes a vocation can be lived effortlessly, when there is enough money, time, and support to be able to work well at it. At other times, however, living out a vocation is more difficult. Circumstances may hinder pursuing your vocation or you may feel as though there are too many demands on you to be able to pursue it.

It is important not to lose sight of that which gives your life fulfillment and meaning.

Do you know what your vocation is? If so, how are you living it?

If you don't know what your vocation is

Do you feel that your life has purpose? In what ways?

Use
your interests, gifts, talents, and strengths to guide you to your vocation.

Know
that the amount of time engaged in pursuing your vocation is less important than your commitment to it.

Recognize
your vocation with a willingness to embrace this part of your best Self.

CHAPTER 4

Sacred Space

A wise old owl sat in an oak.
The more he heard, the less he spoke.
The less he spoke, the more he heard.
Why can't we all be like that wise old bird?

Mother Goose nursery rhyme

One chilly, drizzly January Saturday five months after my son was born, I felt I had to get away. I just had to go somewhere alone or I felt as though I would explode. So with the baby safe with Brian, I left. I drove out to the coast, on windy curvy roads that cut across the headlands. I headed toward the beach, a rugged Northern California cold-water beach that was best encountered dressed in jeans and a sweater.

Through the fog and drizzle, I climbed up on a rock and sat watching the waves crash onto the shore and recede in a powerful rhythm.

I hadn't slept through the night since the baby had been born. The odors of spit up and rice cereal lingered on my clothes and visions of laundry kept clutching my mind. I kept feeling the almost uncontrollable urge to jump up and meet some vital need: feed the baby, do the laundry, do something that needed doing. I consciously had to make myself sit there. I had to tell myself that it was okay to be there, to stay there.

Gradually the waves' hypnotic rhythm slowed my mind and my body. The urges to jump up were fewer.

My whole being had been starving for this—for the peacefulness, the waves, the stillness, my own thoughts, my own breathing. I'd so needed time on my own, to breathe on my own, think on my own, feel what I felt, and not worry about what the baby felt.

Four hours later, stiff, cold, and smelling a lot less like sour milk and a lot more like salty ocean air, I drove back to the tiny seminary apartment I shared with my husband and my son. Amazingly refreshed, I think I even smiled.

It is still sometimes a struggle for me to get as much sacred space as I need. When I worked full-time and had two small children, there were times when the brief moments alone in the bathroom were the extent of my sacred space. It wasn't nearly enough and my spirit cried out for more.

I know I desperately need time alone, time to myself, time to get centered and reconnect with myself, to reconnect with the sacred within me without the externals crowding in.

I've learned that if I don't have sacred space, I do not do well. Irritable, unclear about what I want or what I'm doing, I lose sight of the sacred that resides within me.

Sacred space is a crucial ingredient for a healthy and balanced spiritual life. Just as taking quiet time to be thankful before a meal allows us to enjoy the meal just a bit more, sacred space allows us time to reconnect with what is important in our lives.

Defining Sacred Space

Sacred space quiets our bodies and minds so we can know our Soul. Whatever you do to quiet your mind and body to connect with what is holy and true, to know your Soul, and to know God is sacred space.

Our fast-paced, fast-food, cell-phone culture often demands constant motion and a hectic pace. Yet such constant activity can be deceptive. Our frenetic speed swirls around us and clouds our ability to see and know our Selves, just as swimming in a lake can disturb the sediment and obscure the swimmer's ability to see clearly.

Our frenzied pace and constant activity can make us feel as though our lives are full—that we are accomplishing a lot—that we are getting somewhere—that life is complete.

Finding sacred space is a way to let the constant motion and hectic pace in our lives settle so we can see our Selves clearly, so we can know our soul, so we can connect to that which is holy, sacred, and good.

There are many words used to describe what is holy and true. Different religious and spiritual traditions have their own ways of describing what is sacred. Some call it God. Other names (and this is not a complete list) are the still small voice, the Divine Spark, the Mystery, the Source, the Kingdom of God, the Infinite, the Universe, the fully human, the true self, the Holy Spirit, Higher Power, Living Energy, Allah.

Religious and spiritual traditions have many different ways to practice sacred space. Quiet meditation, prayer, prayer beads, yoga, chanting, and t'ai chi are traditionally religious ways of practicing sacred space and reconnecting with the sacred. Sacred space can also be found in long contemplative walks, sitting by the ocean or on top of a mountain, or carving out a physical space intended for quiet reflection.

Your Exploration

Answer the questions that follow in the space provided.

Which words do *you* use to describe that which is holy and true?

How well does that name (or do those names) work for you?

You may be using a practice that has traditionally been in the religious realm or you may be bringing sacred space into your life through less traditional means. Some ways of practicing sacred space include being in nature, breathing, lighting a candle, sitting still. Anything you do to quiet your body and mind to put you in touch with a deeper reality can be sacred space.

What did you learn about sacred space while you were growing up? (Think about words or messages from parents, significant people in your life, religious teachings as well as actions you observed.)

Who do you know who seems connected to his or her inner sense of what is holy and true?

What practices does this person incorporate in his or her life to connect with the sacred and good?

What do *you* do to quiet your body and mind and connect with a deeper reality (retreat, meditate, pray, light a candle, breathe, sit still)?

How well do these activities honor what is sacred for you?

How often do you engage in these activities?

We need to let the frenzy of our lives settle and quiet
    so we can see our Selves clearly,
        so we can know our soul,
            and reconnect to the holy within.
        When the sediment settles, we can know who We are.

Give yourself the gift of sacred space.

CHAPTER 5

Ritual and Tradition

*In Anatevka we have traditions for everything—
how to eat, how to sleep, how to work, how to
wear clothes. You may ask, "How did this tradition
get started?" I'll tell you, I don't know. But it's tradition!
And because of our traditions, each one of us knows
who he is and what God expects him to do.*

Tevye, Fiddler on the Roof

Ritual

Even though I hadn't been involved with church for five years, when my father died, I turned to the church for guidance and support.

My father had been in declining health for many years. His last four years were spent in a convalescent hospital after my mother could no longer care for him at home. He had Parkinson's disease, causing difficulty with his movements and speech. He also had dementia, possibly caused by the Parkinson's, or possibly "just" dementia. He grew thinner and thinner, until with his dementia and physical decline, we could barely recognize the vital, classical music—loving, sailing, physician who was my dad.

His final physical struggle was with pneumonia. My brother and I, and Brian and the kids rushed down to be with him for his last few days. With my mother, we sat with him as he slipped into unconsciousness, his pain eased with morphine. His breathing slowed, until it finally stopped. It was as peaceful and calm a death as one could hope for. I was honored to be with him as he moved out of this life.

His memorial service was to be at his home church in San Anselmo. The week before the service, friends from church brought food. There were calls of concern and flowers. The current pastor, who didn't know my father very well, spent time getting to know us and through us, to know my father.

The service was a wonderful remembrance of him and his life. People shared stories—including one woman who called on my dad to deliver her teenage daughter's baby, and help put it up for adoption. Another woman shared how my dad helped them adopt a child, as they were unable to have children. We sang, cried, grieved, and remembered.

I needed the ritual the church provided, the guidance from the pastor, the loving concern of the members. I appreciated the opportunity publicly and formally to acknowledge the loss of my father. The church provided the gift of ritual for me, for our family, and for his community.

Tradition

We moved from Wisconsin to California during my son's first grade year. On his last day of kindergarten, we took him out for ice cream to celebrate the end of the year. As he finished first grade in a new school, again on his last day of class, we took him out for ice cream to celebrate.

During the following summer, we moved to the small rural town. At the end of second grade, he asked, "Are we going to go out for ice cream on my last day, like we do every year?" I was stunned at how my six-year-old son had transformed this small event into tradition.

We all need repeated celebrations or actions that remind us of who we are. My son's voicing the desire for an ice-cream outing to celebrate the end of the school year was a way he felt connected to "how *we* do things." He recognized that our family celebrated the end of a school year in this way, and he wanted to make sure it continued. It was a wonderful reminder to me how important tradition is.

Defining Ritual and Tradition

When life passages are honored with ritual and our identity is grounded in tradition, our spiritual practice is richer and has more meaning. Just as using elegant china can make a mere meal into a memorable event, so can ritual and tradition adorn our life passages and affirm our identity, honoring ourselves through this vital spiritual practice.

Institutional religion is often good at providing ritual and tradition in people's lives, offering a spiritual rhythm to religious participants. Many people who are not otherwise connected to a religious institution seek the support of organized religion to honor significant life events.

Ritual provides us with the framework to help us spiritually honor the profound changes in our lives. Tradition provides the structure to help us honor our identity on a deep level.

Ritual

Honoring life transitions or changes, rituals acknowledge that life has altered because a change has occurred.

For instance, a wedding is a ritual that recognizes that two people have made a conscious choice to share their lives. The wedding ritual is for the bride and groom of course. But the ritual also helps the friends and family support and affirm the couple, publicly acknowledging and spiritually honoring that life has changed. The wedding is an important ritual for the couple as well as their community.

The ritual of a funeral acknowledges the death and loss of a loved one. Experiencing the funeral profoundly acknowledges that life has changed for the people who are left. Life is different now because that person is no longer with us. The ritual of the funeral helps us acknowledge the change on a deep spiritual level.

All sorts of life changes can be honored with ritual. Births, deaths, coming of age, commitments, losses—all significant events can be marked and made sacred through ritual.

Rituals speak to the unseen changes that occur inside us, whether or not the change has been a visible one.

Tradition

Traditions remind us who we are. Traditions are the things we do over and over that remind us of our identity—culturally, religiously/spiritually, and with our friends and families. These repeated familiar actions keep us connected to our roots and grounded in our identity.

Some traditions are elaborate and involved, such as large family celebrations. Others may be smaller in scope, such as how a specific dish is prepared, yet they are still significant. Whether large or small, traditions tell us "We do it *this* way because this is who we are."

Organized religion provides tradition and structure for the religious year, honoring events that reflect the identity of those religious practitioners. These are often holiday celebrations (literally "holy-day"), celebrations that remind the followers who they are based on the events they celebrate and remember.

Your Exploration: Ritual

Think about passages or changes that have occurred in your life: births, deaths, marriages, divorce, going to college, getting a job, losing a job, moving, illness, healing, children growing up.

Write down at least three changes or passages you have experienced in your life.

1.

2.

3.

Look at your list again. Have you honored those passages with ritual?

1.

2.

3.

How did the presence of ritual affect the significance of those events for you?

Your Exploration: Tradition

Think **about** some of the traditions you incorporate into your life (holiday celebrations, birthdays, beginnings or endings of a school or work year, religious observations, family reunions, national holidays, family meals, graduations, traditions honoring your cultural heritage).

Keep in mind that events can have elements of both ritual and tradition. For instance, a graduation may be celebrated as a ritual (ceremonial marking of a life passage) for the person moving on. The celebration of a graduation is also a tradition (something we do over and over to connect us to our identity) for that particular school community.

List traditions in your life that honor your identity with

Family:

Community:

Culture:

Nation:

Religion:

Look again at each tradition you've listed.

Do the traditions you celebrate genuinely honor the essence of who you are?

Family:

Community:

Culture:

Nation:

Religion:

Our spirit calls us to acknowledge the sacredness of the events of our lives:
   beginnings and endings
         gains and losses
               reunions and celebrations.

Ritual and tradition provide a framework through which we can honor our identities and life passages.

CHAPTER 6

Harmony with Nature

She say, my first step from the old white man was trees.
Then air. Then birds. Then other people.
But one day when I was sitting quiet and feeling
like a motherless child, which I was, it came to me:
that feeling of being part of everything,
not separate at all. I knew that if I cut a tree,
my arm would bleed. And I laughed and I cried and
I run all around the house. I just knew what it was.
In fact, when it happen, you can't miss it.

The Color Purple, *Alice Walker*

My challenge with harmony with nature has been with my own bodily awareness. In my family, none of us were athletically gifted or particularly active. We played outside when we were kids, and had physical education in school, and that was about it. While my father was a physician and I felt as though I knew a fair amount about the body clinically, I knew very little about its harmony with mind and spirit.

I began to understand the mind/body/spirit connection when I started yoga in 2000. I originally started yoga as a way to become physically strong and more flexible. When I started, I was looking for physical results.

During these last few years in California, Brian and I were working full-time, parenting our two children, and trying to keep the house up. My father's health was declining, which also was a constant concern.

At the same time, my work at the social service agency was getting more stressful. Personnel issues were difficult and needed resolution, and the threat of layoff loomed for more than a year. Staff left for other jobs and I was promoted. Faced with trying to deliver a quality program, needing to resolve some personnel and budgetary issues, and wanting desperately to prevent layoffs, my stress level increased. Threats of losing funding and of not finding future funding hovered low and dark. I was having chest pains, though the echocardiogram and other tests pointed to "just" stress.

Even though I was overwhelmed and stressed, I realized that I was making the Tuesday evening yoga class a priority in my schedule.

In yoga class I focused on my breathing, trying to breathe deep into my belly. I enjoyed feeling so good after yoga class; I felt stretched and worked out as though I'd been massaged from the inside out. As time went on, I found myself taking deep breaths when I felt stressed at work and at home. I felt more connected to my body and to who I was. It reminded me that I was more than the stresses in my life.

Finally in May, as layoff notices were distributed again (including one for me), I realized how exhausted I was. Drained and saddened by the lack of funding for important services, my layoff was almost a relief.

As I reflect on how hard that year of pain and loss, stress and exhaustion was, I am aware of how much yoga helped me survive. Yes, I was exhausted and depleted at the end, but I was intact.

Yoga helped me to slow down, to breathe, to clear out the stresses of clutter of my day. Focusing on the yoga positions helped me reconnect with my physical body. The practice of breathing and stretching as well as reconnecting with my physical body has been important in my spiritual development. I've found that connecting to my body also feeds my spirit.

Being in harmony with nature is about becoming deeply aware of our connectedness to the natural world and our place in it.

Defining Harmony with Nature

From nature we can learn about our connectedness with the cycles of life and death. Through the miracle of growth, bodily awareness, experiencing life with our senses, connecting to our physical selves, experiencing beauty, and being aware of the vastness beyond ourselves, we are able to connect to our spirit on a deeper level.

Being in nature—standing by an ocean, looking at an expanse of stars in the night sky, watching a sunset, being with animals, hiking in the forest, truly seeing a flower—can remind us how connected we are to nature. Allowing and appreciating these experiences feeds our spirit.

Religious traditions address our relationship with nature in a variety of ways. Many religions take their lessons directly from nature, acknowledging its rhythms and flow. Religions also discern the balance between activities that are in harmony with nature and those that are not. Many religions have put their best resources to use creating beautiful artwork, glorious music, and stunning architecture.

To be in harmony with nature is to dissolve our separation from the natural world and discover our place in it.

Your Exploration

Use the space provided to write down your responses to the following questions.

Connecting with our own physical needs can bring us to a larger awareness of our connection with nature. Our own bodily rhythms and needs for rest, exercise, food, and elimination help bring us into harmony with the natural world and with each other.

Physical Needs/Bodily Awareness
Are you aware of your physical needs and rhythms for

1. **Sleep and rest?** (Are you getting enough sleep and rest for your spirit? too much?) Describe your ideal rhythm for sleep and rest.

2. **Exercise?** (Do you include exercise in your life that nurtures your whole self—spiritual as well as physical?) Describe your ideal exercise rhythm.

3. **Eating?** (Do you eat foods that feed your spirit as well as your body?) Describe your ideal rhythm for eating.

4. **Elimination?** (Do you honor your body's natural timetable for elimination?)

(For women) **Are you aware of your body's menstrual rhythms?** (Do you allow yourself to be aware of the patterns of your menstrual cycle?)

Connection with Nature

Think about times you have felt most connected to nature.

Where is it?

When is it?

How are you different when you allow yourself to be fully in harmony with nature?
Complete the following sentence.

When I feel in harmony with nature, I

Beauty, Art, the Senses, and Expressing Emotion

In addition to understanding natural rhythms and connecting with nature, harmony with nature also includes appreciation of beauty and art and experiencing the senses. So often we go through life not seeing, not hearing, and not tasting. Yet deeply feeling the wonder in nature, the joy of music, the rhythm of dance, the glory of beauty, and the ecstasy of enjoying good food enhances our spiritual practice.

Our spirit calls us to experience fully and deeply. By doing so, we understand our nature on a profound and visceral level, deeper than words.

The following areas can be areas of spiritual enjoyment and fulfillment.
Think about *beauty*. Complete the sentences to honor your own experience.

I see beauty when

I think _____ **is beautiful.** (Enter as many responses as you'd like.)

Think about *sex*.

Sex is fulfilling when

Think about *dance*. (Do you dance? What role does dance play in your life? Do you like to watch dance? How are you different when you experience dance?)

When I experience dance, I

Dancing makes me feel

Think about *art*. (Is art important to you? Do you create art? Do you appreciate others' art? Does art speak to you more deeply than words? If so, how? What happens in your body when you experience profound art? What happens to your spirit?)

The types of art that touch me most deeply are

When I experience art that touches me deeply, I

Think about *music*. (Do you create music? What happens in your body when you experience music? What happens to your spirit?)

The type of music that most touches me is

When I genuinely experience music, I

Think about *your laughter*. (When did you last laugh fully and deeply, with genuine enjoyment? Do you laugh enough? Do you laugh too much? Is your laughter constricted in any way?)

Laughter is

When I laugh well, I

Think about your tears and *crying*. (Have you honored your sorrow with tears? When you cry, do you allow yourself to let go and feel the emotions? Do you cry enough? Do you cry too much?)

Crying is

When I cry well, I

Remember a time you really allowed your senses to experience something fully, when the experience seemed to feed your spirit. (Some examples may be taking time to fully enjoy food or drink, allowing music to flood your soul, dancing and feeling connected to your body, finding true intimacy and connection through touch.)

Use the following space to write down enough about the experience to remember it, as well as how you were better because of this experience.

Physical and bodily experiences can
connect us with our spirit on a deep level. Being in
harmony with nature allows us to experience
our physical humanity deeply and fully,
at the same time allowing us to transcend
our physical bodies by connecting us with the spirit.

CHAPTER 7

Community

Losing family obliges us to find our family,
not always our blood,
but family that becomes our blood.

Jamal Wallace, *Finding Forrester*

While I was struggling with being the pastor's wife and feeling ornamental (a "sort-of-included-but-not-truly-recognized" feeling), I was also trying to fit in beyond the pastor's wife role. This was a challenge.

Growing up in the San Francisco Bay area, I was used to meeting people from different places. My relatives were scattered all over the country. As I was growing up, my family made friends with people who also didn't have relatives close by, who were also looking for friends. I was used to starting conversations with people I didn't know by asking where they were from.

I tried to start conversations in this new place that way, too. When I met someone, I asked where they were from. They replied, "Here. Where are *you* from?" The answer implied that I'd asked a weird question, since everyone was from there.

One of the church members told me, "If I didn't go to high school with you, or my parents didn't go to high school with you, then you're a stranger." I felt like a stranger. The church members teased us, calling us "foreigners" and "aliens."

People did not seem to socialize with people outside their families, and rarely left the city to experience other things. Chicago was an hour and a half away, and Milwaukee was a mere twenty minutes away, but even so, some lifetime residents had rarely left their community to see the sights offered in these larger cities.

This attitude of not needing anything or anyone else increased my feelings of separation. I felt as though my authentic self wasn't wanted, understood, or appreciated. I did have a few close friends, but for the entire time we lived there, I felt as though I didn't belong.

We've lived in this new place for over two years now. Already I've connected with a group of writers. We share our love of writing as well as our professional aspirations, providing support, encouragement, and respect to one another. I'm actively exploring other groups I might resonate with, being discriminating but also eager, thirstily drinking in opportunities. It seems as though I've been yearning for this connection, this belonging for a long time.

Defining Community

We are in community when we feel an affinity with someone or with a group of people. We recognize our affinity as we identify with or feel connected to others. This connection can happen through sharing a common past or experiences, pursuing common goals, sharing interests, or recognizing a deep level of connection.

For example, connection that occurs from sharing a common past can be with our family members, longtime friends, and people we went to school with, grew up with, or worked with.

Community can also occur as we identify others who have gone through experiences that are similar to ours—traumatic experiences (illness, natural disaster, war, death, pain, or suffering)—or similar circumstances—parenthood, economic difficulties, and so on. Religions form community in pursuit of the shared goals of their religious expression and shared values. Other examples include political groups, philanthropic groups, and business ventures. People coming together to share interests can also be an expression of community such as sports or activity teams or leagues, book or craft clubs or groups, or music appreciation groups.

As we feel our deep connection and identify with others, our sense of community can extend to larger groups, even if we don't have a personal relationship with each individual. This is evident, for example, when we feel connection with "all Americans" or "women" or even "all of humanity."

People demonstrate or express their connection in a variety of ways. Having an involved family life, serving on a school board, writing a letter in political protest, playing on a soccer team, or traveling to another country to help disaster victims are all expressions of community. We express our connection to those with whom we feel an affinity by how we choose to participate in relationship with them.

As we are more involved with our community, as our relationships within our community become closer and more personal, the quality of those relationships becomes more important. For instance, you may feel an affinity to faraway disaster victims and may send a check as an expression of your human connection with the victims. However, the quality of the relationship between the check writer and the recipients is not an important factor. The quality of the check writer's relationship with her own family members is much more significant because of the proximity and intensity of the relationships. To enrich spiritual life, relationships, whether in groups or between individuals, should demonstrate commitment, acceptance, trust, honesty, respect, and mutuality. Diversity is accepted within the limits of that community's common purpose.

We recognize that we share our lives with each other in community, sharing our common humanity and working toward relationships that support and nurture us to become our best selves.

Your Exploration

Name the ten people closest to you and most important in your life.

1.   6.

2.   7.

3.   8.

4.   9.

5.   10.

Name five groups in which you participate and feel the greatest connection.

1.

2.

3.

4.

5.

Of those individuals and groups you named, which do you feel connected to because of

•**Shared interests** (professional pursuits, hobbies, sports, etc.)

•**Shared history** (family members, longtime friends, former colleagues, friends from school, etc.)

•**Shared experience** (moving, death, loss, trauma, illness, healing, divorce, physical challenges, etc.)

•**Pursuit of a common goal** (coworkers; a specific religious or spiritual group; political, social, or economic groups; task forces; boards or organizations on which you serve, etc.)

The quality of the relationships is important as well as the feeling of connection.

Reflect on the quality of the relationship and how well it represents your sense of connection. **As you look at the relationships in your life (with groups or individuals), in which relationships do you feel**

•**A shared sense of commitment?**

•Mutual acceptance?

•Respect?

•Trust?

•Able to share your differences and be accepted for your point of view?

Again, as you look at the relationships in your life, which relationships do you NOT feel

•A shared sense of commitment?

•Mutual acceptance?

•Respect?

•Trust?

•Able to share your differences and be accepted for your point of view?

Which relationships embody mutuality—that is, a shared sense of leadership and participation—rather than power over or domination of others?

Our spirit longs for a sense of connection with others, a sense of belonging.
We all need community…
…relationships with those with whom we have common purpose…
…trusting, respectful, and committed relationships….
…in which we are active participants and have satisfying roles…
Connection.
Sharing our lives.
Mutual support.

Community.

Chapter 8

Your Spiritual Life

*There's no place to go to be separated from
the spiritual, so perhaps one might say that
the spiritual is that realm of human experience
which religion attempts to connect us to through
dogma and practice. Sometimes it succeeds and
sometimes it fails. Religion is a bridge to the
spiritual—but the spiritual lies beyond religion.
Unfortunately in seeking the spiritual we may
become attached to the bridge rather
than crossing over it.*

Rachel Naomi Remen, M.D.

The previous chapters provided an in-depth look at each of the seven areas of spiritual practice. Here again is an opportunity for you to take the assessment, perhaps resulting in different, more revealing scores than when you took it at the beginning of the book.

The Assessment, Again

For each question, rank your level of satisfaction with a number from 1 to 10. A score of 1 represents very low satisfaction while a score of ten represents a high level of satisfaction. Remember that this is *your* perception and *your* sense of satisfaction with these areas of your life.

Section 1
How satisfied are you with
_____1. The presence of compassion in your closest relationships?
_____2. The amount of time and energy you feel you can commit to compassionate activities on behalf of others?
_____3. Your openness and ability to accept help from others in your times of need?

Section II
How satisfied are you with
_____4. Your chosen beliefs and values to guide you through life?
_____5. How well your beliefs are integrated into your daily living?
_____6. Your ability to live your life in keeping with your deepest values?

Section III
How satisfied are you with
_____7. Your sense of purpose and meaning for your life?
_____8. The feeling that you have gifts and abilities that benefit others?
_____9. The amount of time and energy you spend in activities that give you meaning, pleasure, and a sense of accomplishment?

Section IV

How satisfied are you with

_____10. The amount of unscheduled, relaxing time in your life?

_____11. How much you engage in reflection and contemplation (meditation, prayer, yoga, silent walks, etc.)?

_____12. Your sense of connection to the most sacred part of life (God, soul, true Self, ground of being, source of life, higher power, The Force, etc.)?

Section V

How satisfied are you with

_____13. The level of tradition in your life that ties you to those closest to you and to your community?

_____14. The rituals in your life to convey a sense of spiritual meaning during life transitions?

_____15. Your ability to honor and commemorate meaningful events in your own life?

Section VI

How satisfied are you with

_____16. Your ability to keep mind/body/spirit in harmony and balance?

_____17. The amount of time you spend in deeply pleasurable activities (music, massage, enjoyment of food, sexual intimacy, being in nature)?

_____18. Your body, its rhythms and your physical activities?

Section VII

How satisfied are you with

_____19. The amount of acceptance you feel from those most important to you?

_____20. Your comfort in sharing your thoughts, feelings, ideas, and opinions with those closest to you?

_____21. The level of honesty, trust, and commitment in your relationships?

In each section of three questions, add your scores. For example, if for question 1, you scored your satisfaction level at a 7, and for question 2, you scored your satisfaction level at a 6, and for question 3, you scored your satisfaction level at an 8, your total score for that section would be 21.

Do this for each of the sections. List your totals for each of the sections.

Section I	_____ Compassion
Section II	_____ Worldview
Section III	_____ Vocation
Section IV	_____ Sacred Space
Section V	_____ Ritual and Tradition
Section VI	_____ Harmony with Nature
Section VII	_____ Community

The highest possible score in a section is 30; the lowest is 3.

We feel better and function better when our diet is healthy and balanced, when we are aware of our nutritional needs and discover our own most healthy eating habits. In the same way, our overall well-being is also enhanced when our spiritual practice is balanced and fulfilling.

Finding your spiritual life is about finding what works for you, about your ability to draw on resources you have access to in order to make your spiritual life as balanced and fulfilling as you want it to be.

In this chapter we'll look again at each of the seven areas. Use this as an opportunity to reflect on each domain and plan concrete things you can do to make each area more healthy for you.

Enhancing Areas

As you discover areas in your spiritual life that you want to enhance or develop more fully, commit realistically to developing them. Be intentional about it, but not obsessive. Just being aware of the area and having a desire to improve its presence in your life is a huge step toward improvement.

Allow yourself to move toward your own spiritual life with increased awareness and gentle intention.

Discovering your spiritual life means being more in tune with your own story, your preferences, and your values. It means becoming more aware of what brings **meaning, purpose,** and **connection** to you.

Compassion

If you want to enhance the area of compassion in your life, observe your life for a week or two. Notice who expresses compassion to you. Notice to whom you express compassion. Ask yourself if your actions are borne of genuine compassion or out of guilt or obligation. Notice the ways you express compassion that feel genuine to you.

Examine your own background. What grounding do you have for compassion? What roots it? What is the purpose of it, in your life, in your belief system?

Complete the sentences to reflect your experience.

I ranked my satisfaction level of compassion as _____ (from the assessment)

Compassion is most satisfying for me when

Compassion is least satisfying for me when

To honor compassion in my life, in the next week, I will

In the next month, I will

Allow yourself to notice the many expressions of *compassion* in your life.

Worldview

If you want to enhance your worldview, you may realize that you not have been aware of how your beliefs, values, and experiences have shaped you, or you may find that your life hasn't been a reflection of values you embrace.

Look for ways you can live out your values, even if they are small. Pay attention to family members and childhood friends to get a more accurate picture of the beliefs and values present in your upbringing. Notice how your beliefs, values, and experiences have shaped you. Recognize how the life you live is an expression of your values as well as how it isn't.

Complete the sentences to reflect your experiences and your intention.

I ranked my satisfaction level of worldview as _____ (from the assessment)

The most satisfying aspect of my worldview is

The least satisfying aspect of my worldview is

To honor worldview in my life, in the next week, I will

In the next month, I will

Honor and recognize your *worldview*.

Vocation

If you want to enhance your level of satisfaction with how well you are living your vocation, I encourage you to step back and observe your life. Recognize what it is that brings you delight. Notice what are you engaged in when you lose track of time. You may discover that little of your time fits your vocation. You may have to remember back to younger days. Sometimes what we loved in our childhood can help us remember interests, gifts, and strengths that we've forgotten in the world we believe we are "supposed" to live in as an adult. What did you love to do as a child? What did you spend hours doing? What piqued your interest, and made you want to learn more and do it longer? What activity made you feel alive?

Complete the sentences to reflect your experiences and your intention.

I ranked my satisfaction level of vocation as _____ (from the assessment)

Vocation is most satisfying for me when

Vocation is least satisfying for me when

To honor vocation in my life, in the next week, I will

In the next month, I will

Allow time to live out your *vocation*.

Sacred Space

If you want to enhance sacred space in your life, you may have found that your life is so full that you don't have any time for personal reflection. This is a challenge in our busy American culture. Notice opportunities in your life where you could include sacred space. Notice when and where in your life you feel connected to what is sacred within you. Notice how you refer to what is sacred for you.

Complete the sentences to reflect your experience and your intention.

I ranked my satisfaction level of sacred space as _____ (from the assessment)

Sacred space is most satisfying for me when

Sacred space is least satisfying for me when

To honor sacred space in my life, in the next week, I will

In the next month, I will

Embrace the chance to get quiet with *sacred space*.

Ritual and Tradition

If you want to develop ritual and tradition in your life, you may want to reflect on your life/family history. Have there been a lot of changes? Have you changed religious perspectives and practices, perhaps not participating in religion as much as you used to? If so, you may want to reflect on ways you can develop rituals and traditions that accurately reflect where you are now in your life. What traditions can you start, or do you already do, that accurately reflect your identity now?

Complete the sentences to reflect your experiences and your intention.

I ranked my satisfaction level of ritual and tradition as _____ (from the assessment)

Ritual and tradition is most satisfying for me when

Ritual and tradition is least satisfying for me when

To honor ritual and tradition in my life, in the next week, I will

In the next month, I will

Give yourself the opportunity to honor your life changes and identity with *ritual and tradition*.

Harmony with Nature

If you want to enhance your harmony with nature, you may need to incorporate and be more conscious of time in nature, your bodily needs and experiences, or take time to experience beauty, art, and music, as well as to make life enjoyment a priority.

Complete the sentences to reflect your experiences and your intention.

I ranked my satisfaction level of harmony with nature as _____ (from the assessment)

   Harmony with nature is most satisfying for me when

   Harmony with nature is least satisfying for me when

   To honor harmony with nature in my life, in the next week, I will

   In the next month, I will

Be aware of the opportunities to experience *harmony with nature.*

Community

If you want to develop your community, you may want to reflect on those with whom you have an affinity, or those with whom you identify. You may need to become more aware of those with whom you have an affinity. This may also be an opportunity for you to examine your relationships to see how healthy they are. You may have to do some personal work and reflection if there are patterns in your life that have resulted in unhealthy community. You also may want to reflect on your sphere of participation within your communities, examining your role and how you want to be present in each set of relationships. Be aware of toxic people in your life, and decide how you will manage their effect on you.

Complete each sentence to honor your experience and your intention.

I ranked my satisfaction level of community as _____ (from the assessment)

Community is most satisfying for me when

Community is least satisfying for me when

To honor community in my life, in the next week, I will

In the next month, I will

Appreciate your *community*.

Bibliography

The Artist's Way, Julie Cameron, 1992, G.P. Putnam's Sons.

The Dance of Anger, Harriet Goldhor Lerner, Ph.D., 1985, Harper & Row Publishers.

The Different Drum: Community Making and Peace, M. Scott Peck, 1987, Touchstone (Simon and Schuster).

From Beginning to End: The Rituals of Our Lives, Robert Fulghum, 1995, Random House, New York.

Hymns to an Unknown God: Awakening the Spirit in Everyday Life, Sam Keen, 1994, Bantam Books, New York.

Kitchen Table Wisdom, Rachel Naomi Remen, M.D., 1996, Riverhead Books (Putnam).

Man's Search for Meaning, Viktor E. Frankl, 1959, Pocket Books.

My Grandfather's Blessings, Rachel Naomi Remen, M.D., 2000, Riverhead Books, (Penguin Putnam).

The Power of Myth, Joseph Campbell (book and video series).

The Reinvention of Work, Matthew Fox, 1994, Harper Collins.

The Satellite Sisters' Uncommon Senses, Liz, Sheila, Monica, Julie and Lian Dolan, 2001, Riverhead Books.

A Spirituality Named Compassion, Matthew Fox, 1979, Harper Collins

Sunbeams, quotations collected by Sy Safransky, 1990, North Atlantic Books.

Transplanted Man, Sanjay Nigam, 2002, William Morrow.

A User's Guide to the Brain, John J. Ratey, M.D., 2001, Vintage Books, New York.

The Wisdom of the Body, Sherwin B. Nuland, 1997, Knopf, New York.

Filmography

About a Boy—**community** (dir: Chris Weitz and Paul Weitz, 2002)

American Beauty—**harmony with nature** (dir: Sam Mendes, 1999)

Babette's Feast—**harmony with nature** (dir: Gabriel Axel, 1988)

Barbershop—**community, vocation** (dir: Tim Story, 2002)

Billy Elliot—**vocation** (dir: Stephen Daldry, 2000)

The Castle—**community** (dir: Rob Sitch, 1999)

Changing Lanes—**worldview** (dir: Roger Michell, 2002)

Chariots of Fire—**vocation, harmony with nature** (dir: Hugh Hudson, 1981)

Citizen Kane—**worldview** (dir: Orson Welles, 1941)

Crimson Tide—**worldview** (dir: Tony Scott, 1995)

Dead Man Walking—**compassion** (dir: Tim Robbins, 1995)

Don Juan DeMarco—**harmony with nature** (dir: Jeremy Leven, 1995)

The Elephant Man—**compassion** (dir: David Lynch, 1980)

Father of the Bride—**ritual (and tradition)** (dir: Charles Shyer, 1991)

Fiddler on the Roof—**tradition (and ritual)** (dir: Norman Jewison, 1971)

Field of Dreams—**worldview, community** (dir: Phil Alden Robinson, 1989)

Finding Forrester—**community** (dir: Gus Van Sant, 2000)

The Fly—**compassion** (dir: David Cronenberg, 1986)

Galaxy Quest—**vocation** (dir: Dean Parisot, 1999)

Garden State—**harmony with nature** (dir: Zach Braff, 2004)

Gattaca—**vocation** (dir: Andrew Niccol, 1997)

Groundhog Day—**worldview, compassion** (dir: Harold Ramis, 1993)

Hotel Rwanda—**compassion** (dir: Terry George, 2004)

The Incredibles—**vocation** (dir: Brad Bird, 2004)

It's a Wonderful Life—**community, vocation** (dir: Frank Capra, 1946)

Little Voice—**vocation** (dir: Mark Herman, 1998)

The Matrix—**worldview** (dir: Andy Wachowski and Larry Wachowski, 1999)

Million Dollar Baby—**compassion** (dir: Clint Eastwood, 2004)

The Mission—**compassion** (dir: Roland Joffe, 1986)

My Big Fat Greek Wedding—**community** (dir: Joel Zwick, 2002)

Nell—**harmony with nature, worldview** (dir: Michael Apted, 1994)

A Perfect Storm—**vocation** (dir: Wolfgang Peterson, 2000)

Pieces of April—**community, ritual and tradition** (dir: Peter Hedges, 2004)

Pleasantville—**worldview** (dir: Gary Ross, 1999)

Ray—**vocation** (dir: Taylor Hackford, 2004)

The Razor's Edge—**sacred space** (dir: John Byrum, 1984)

A River Runs Through It—**worldview** (dir: Robert Redford, 1992)

Saved!—**worldview, compassion** (dir: Brian Dannelly, 2004)

Schindler's List—**compassion** (dir: Steven Spielberg, 1993)

Spiderman—**vocation** (dir: Sam Raimi, 2002)

Strictly Ballroom—**vocation** (dir: Baz Luhrmann, January 1996)

The Turning Point—**vocation** (dir: Herbert Ross, 1977)

Whale Rider—**vocation** (dir: Niki Caro, 2002)

The Center for Public Spirituality is committed to helping people honor religious diversity and spiritual connection. The Center offers organizational consulting, keynotes, workshops, and a variety of other resources. We invite you to come to the Web site.
www.public-spirituality.com

One of our next projects is a book currently titled
One Nation: Portraits of America's Spiritual Expression.
If you would like to submit your written description of your experience(s) in one of the seven areas to be considered for inclusion in *One Nation*, see the Web site for submission guidelines and updates on the book's progress.

978-0-595-34205-1
0-595-34205-1

CPSIA information can be obtained at www.ICGtesting.com
Printed in the USA
LVOW051020160412

277783LV00004B/76/A

9 780595 342051